The Child

The Child

by
HUBERT BERMONT

photographs by
SHELLEY LANGSTON

AN ESSANDESS® SPECIAL EDITION

New York

THE CHILD

SBN 671-10072-6

Copyright, ©, 1965 by Hubert Bermont
and Shelley Langston.
All rights reserved.
Published by ESSANDESS SPECIAL EDITIONS, a division of Simon &
Schuster, Inc., 630 Fifth Avenue, New York, N.Y. 10020.
Printed in the U.S.A.

Opening quotation from *Markings,* by Dag Hammarskjöld.
Translated by Leif Sjoberg and W. H. Auden. Reprinted
with permission of the publisher. Copyright, ©, 1964 by
Alfred A. Knopf, Inc. and Faber and Faber, Ltd.

THIRD PRINTING

CHILDHOOD

"To exist in the fleet joy of becoming...."

Dag Hammarskjöld

MARKINGS

The Child

A child?

There is a time at the beginning
when your child is very close to you,
never going far from your side.

This is the time when, completely innocent,
a child asks only to love and to be loved.

This is the time
when a child reaches joyfully

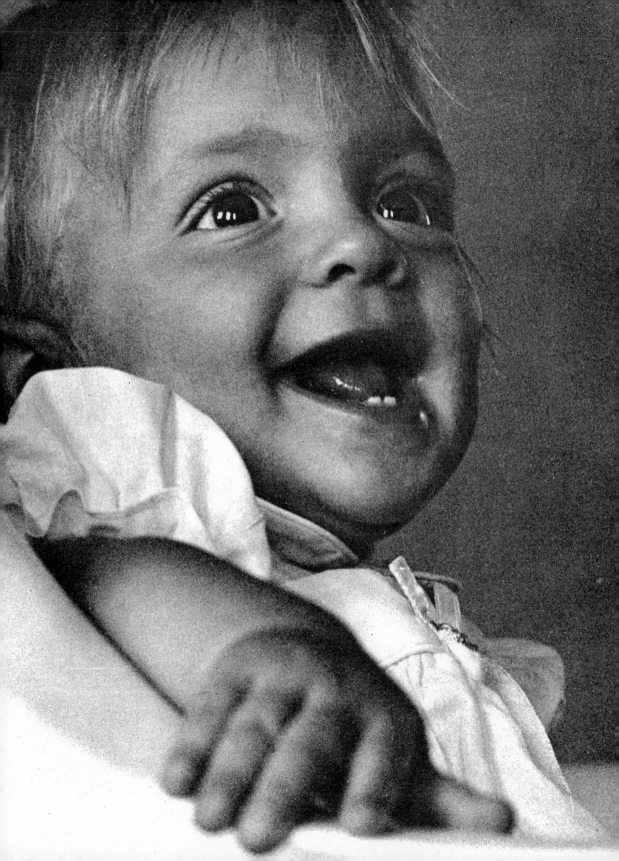

toward a smile and a touch.

This is a time when a child goes naked.

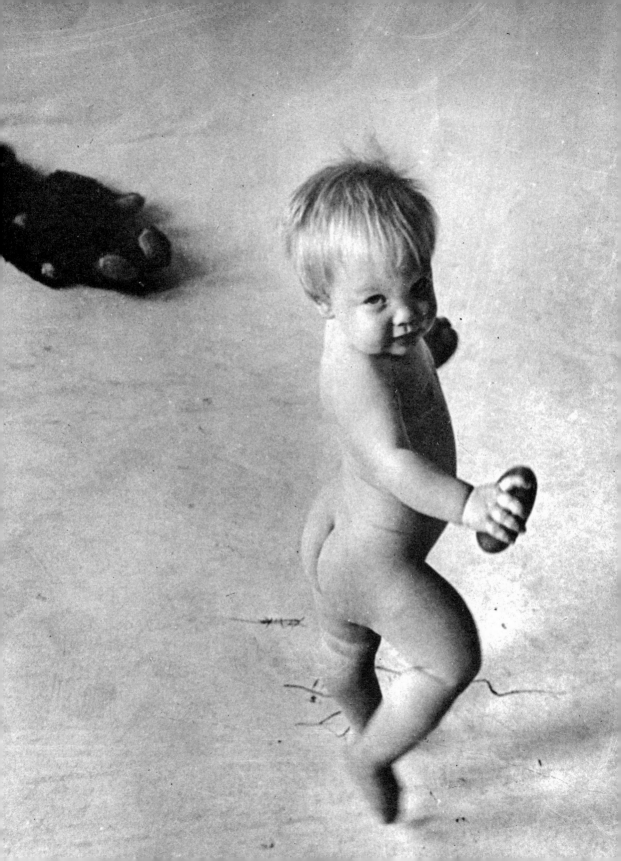

And he asks you to put on nothing,

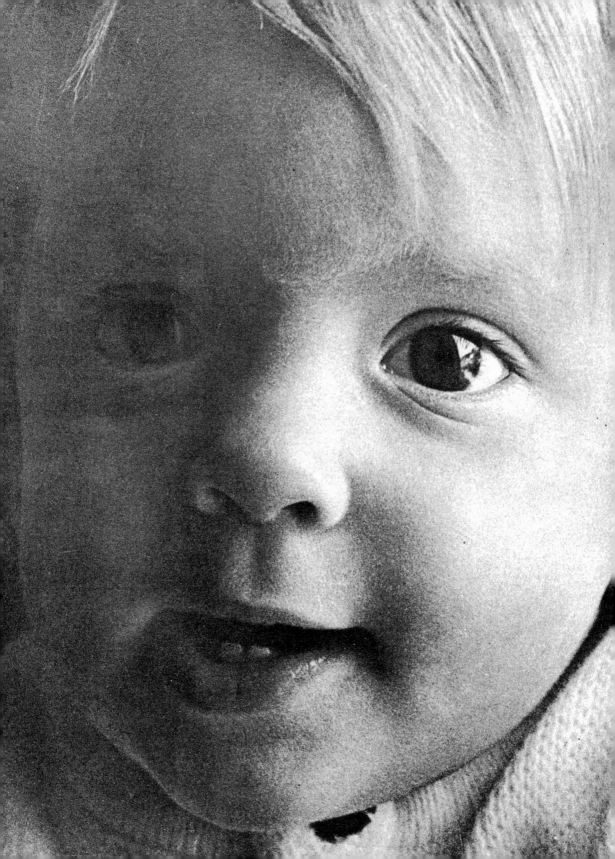

to be just what you really are.

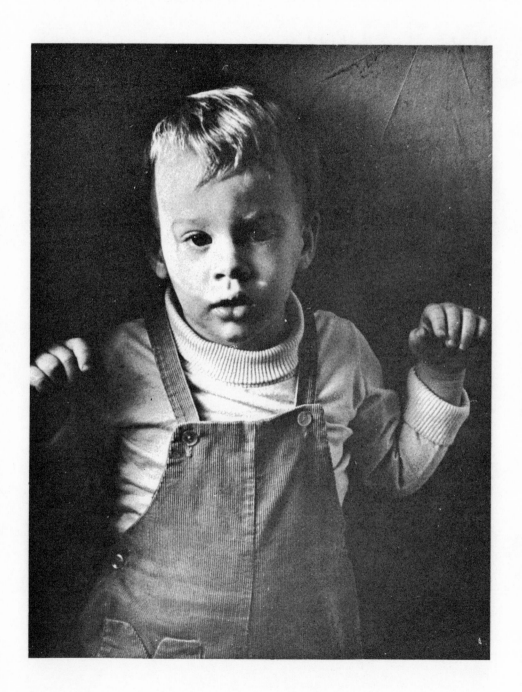

Nothing can be hidden
from the soft eyes of a child.

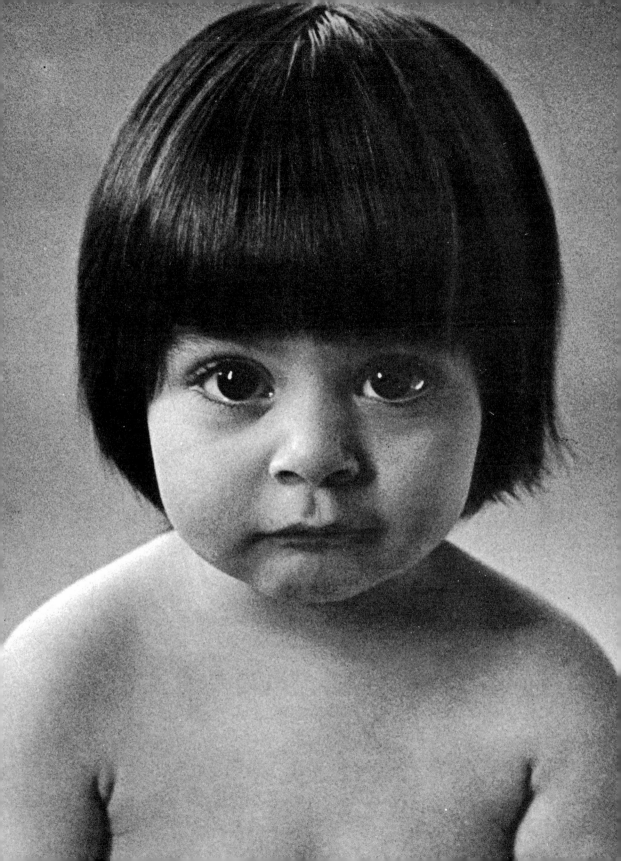

Everything must be out in the open between you two.

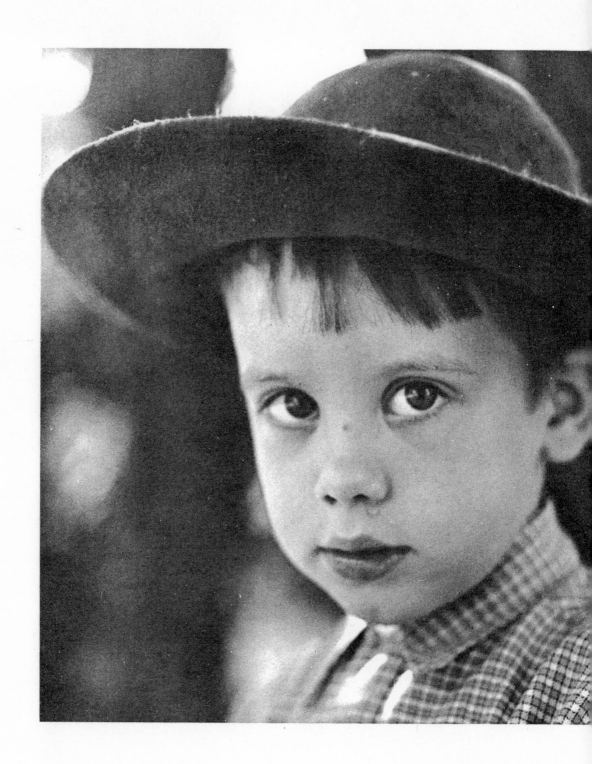

There comes a time of first looking,

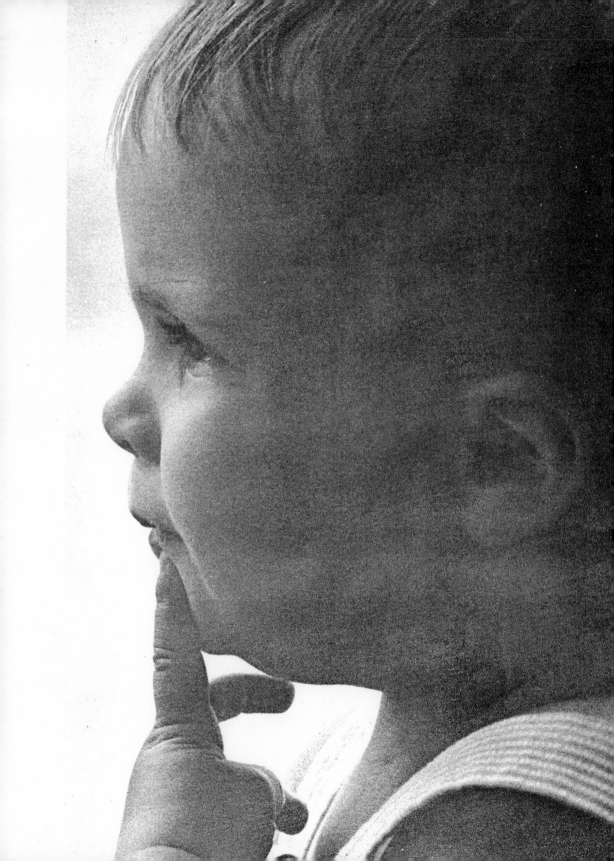

of first wandering,

of stretching high,

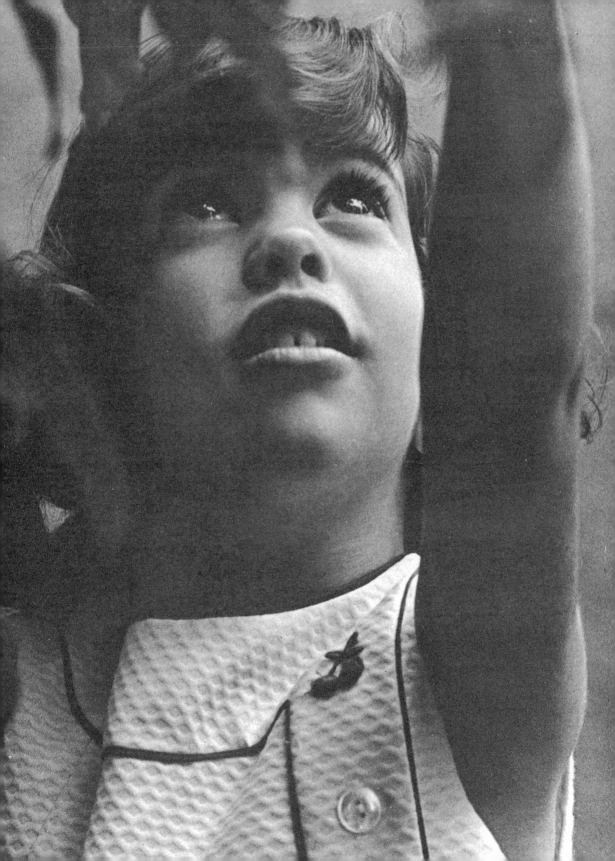

searching,

sniffing,

and discovering the wonder of the world.

This is the time
when small fingers touch lightly,

delicately raising beauty to young lips.

This is the time for careful looking,

for happy surprises,

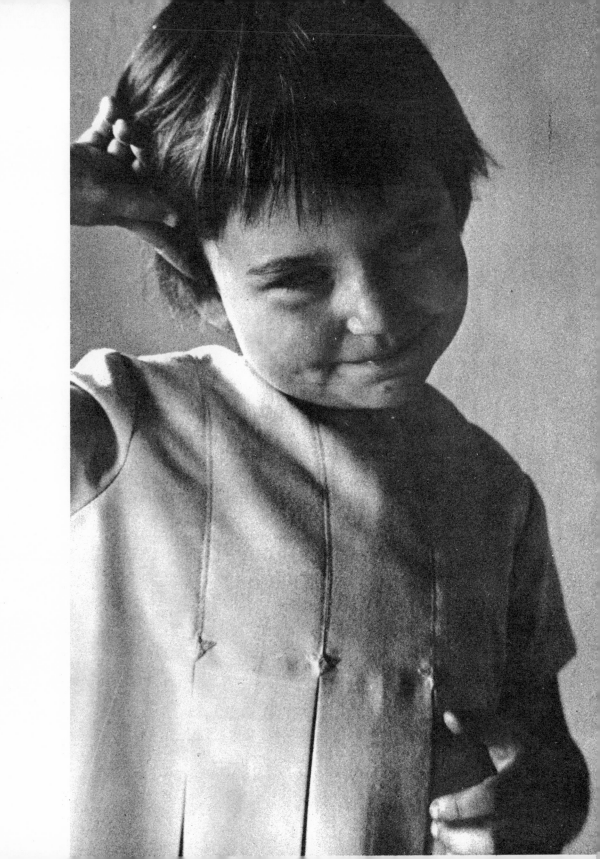

for reveling in the newness of things,

when all the world is fresh,

and its freshness brings only joy.

There is a time for sadness,

children's quiet sorrow.

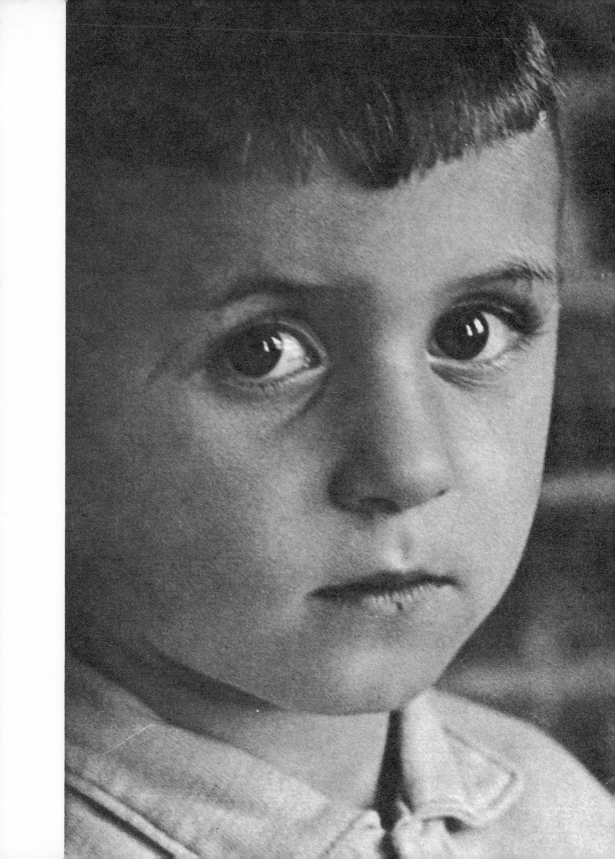

This is the time for standing apart,

and finding a place far away

to be lonely, all alone.

This is the time of shy longing,

and clinging to what is already known,

when a child is no longer
happy to explore the world alone.

This is the time of yearning

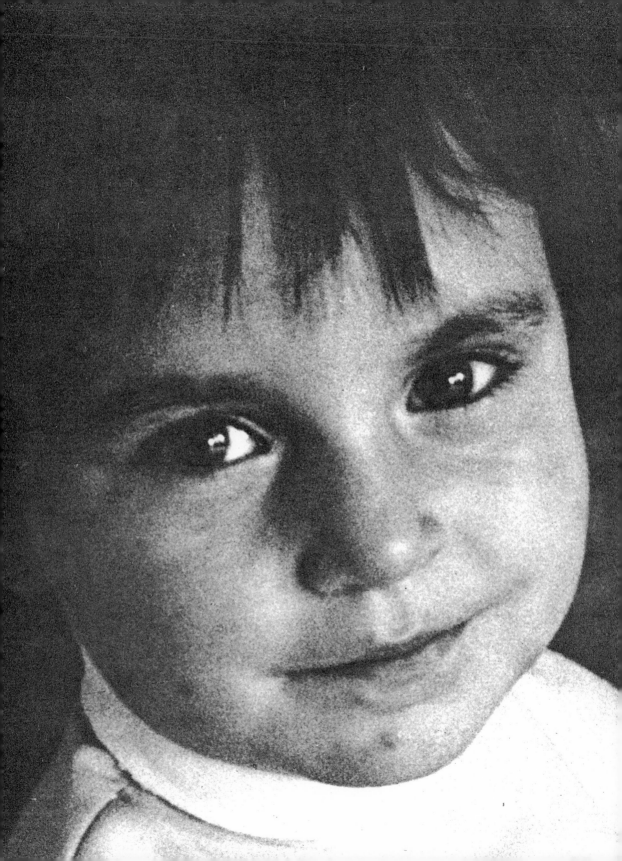

for a friend,

to be close to, so very close,

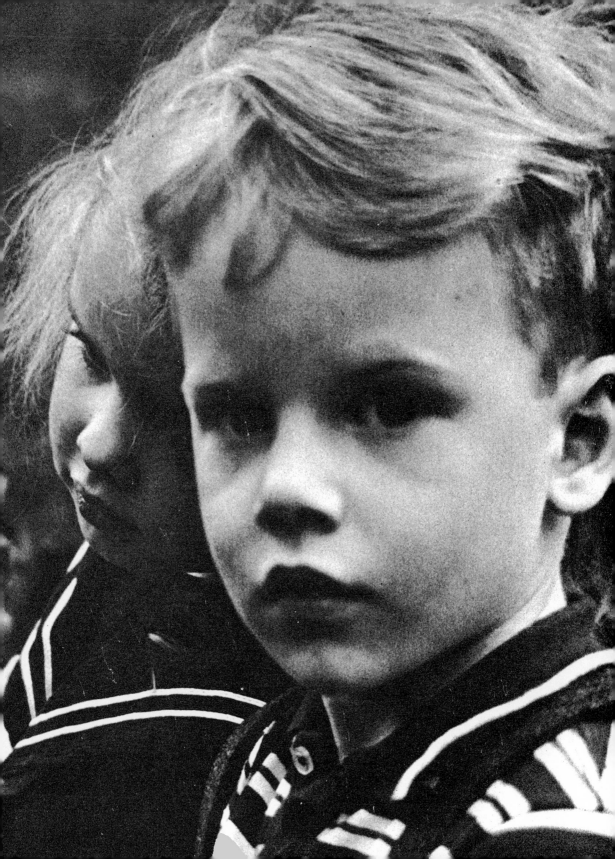

a friend to go wandering with, hand in hand.